THE NOVEL
CAROL-SINGERS' CC

CW01573104

50 TRADITIONAL CAROLS FOR CHRISTMAS

NOVELLO

Contents

A great and mighty wonder

Music: Traditional
Words: St Germanus
English Translation: John Neale

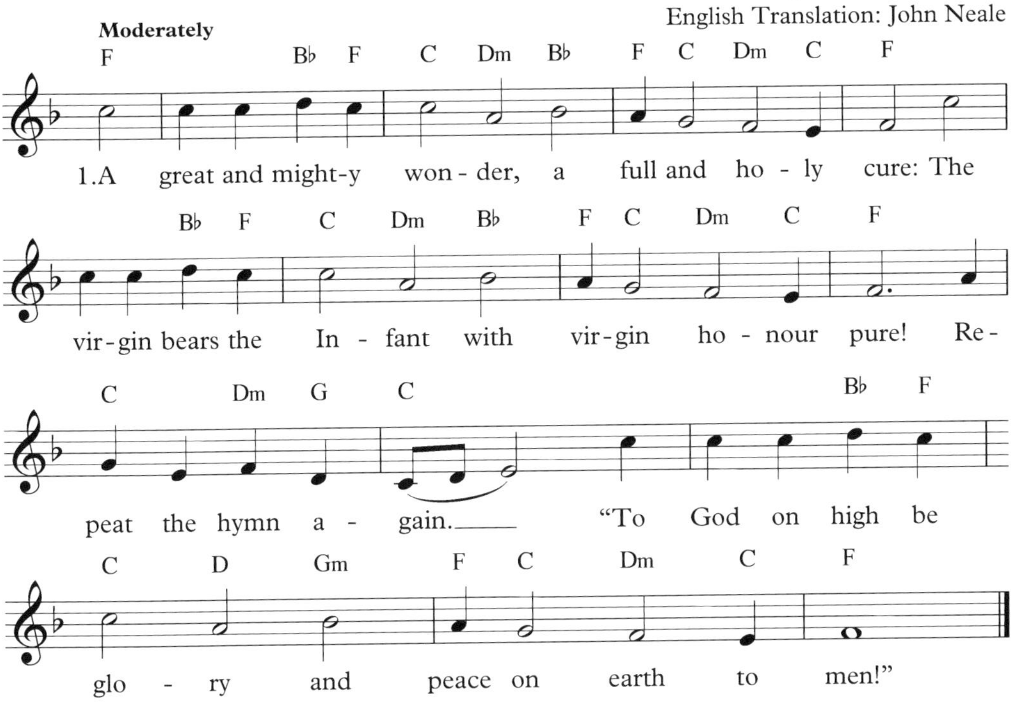

1. A great and mighty wonder, a full and holy cure:
The virgin bears the Infant with virgin honour pure!
Repeat the hymn again: "To God on high be glory
And peace on earth to men!"

2. The Word becomes incarnate and yet remains on high,
And cherubim sing anthems to shepherds from the sky.
Repeat the hymn again: "To God on high be glory
And peace on earth to men!"

3. While thus they sing your Monarch, those bright angelic bands,
Rejoice, ye vales and mountains, ye oceans, clap your hands.
Repeat the hymn again: "To God on high be glory
And peace on earth to men!"

4. Since all He comes to ransom, by all be He adored,
The Infant born in Bethl'em, the Saviour and the Lord.
Repeat the hymn again: "To God on high be glory
And peace on earth to men!"

Angels from the realms of glory

Music: Traditional
Words: James Montgomery

Brightly

1. Angels, from the realms of glory,
Wing your flight o'er all the earth;
Ye who sang creation's story,
Now proclaim Messiah's birth:

Gloria in excelsis Deo!
Gloria in excelsis Deo!

2. Shepherds in the fields abiding,
Watching o'er your flocks by night,
God with man is now residing;
Yonder shines the infant Light:

3. Sages, leave your contemplations;
Brighter visions beam afar:
Seek the great Desire of nations;
Ye have seen His natal star:

4. Saints before the altar bending,
Watching long in hope and fear,
Suddenly the Lord, descending,
In His temple shall appear:

As with gladness men of old

Music: Conrad Kocher
Words: William Chatterton Dix

1. As with gladness men of old
Did the guiding star behold,
As with joy they hailed its light,
Leading onward, beaming bright:
So, most glorious Lord, may we
Evermore be led to Thee.

2. As with joyful steps they sped
To that lowly manger bed,
There to bend the knee before
Him Whom Heaven and earth adore;
So may we with willing feet
Ever seek Thy mercy seat.

3. As they offered gifts most rare
At that manger rude and bare;
So may we with holy joy,
Pure and free from sin's alloy,
All our costliest treasures bring,
Christ, to Thee, our heavenly King.

4. Holy Jesus, every day
Keep us in the narrow way;
And, when earthly things are past,
Bring our ransomed souls at last
Where they need no star to guide,
Where no clouds Thy glory hide.

5. In the heavenly country bright,
Need they no created light;
Thou its Light, its Joy, its Crown,
Thou its Sun which goes not down;
There forever may we sing
Alleluias to our King!

Away in a manger

Moderately

Words and music: Traditional

1. Away in a manger,
No crib for a bed,
The little Lord Jesus
Laid down His sweet head.
The stars in the bright sky
Looked down where He lay,
The little Lord Jesus
Asleep on the hay.

2. The cattle are lowing,
The baby awakes,
But little Lord Jesus
No crying He makes.
I love thee, Lord Jesus!
Look down from the sky,
And stay by my side
Until morning is nigh.

3. Be near me, Lord Jesus,
I ask Thee to stay
Close by me forever,
And love me, I pray.
Bless all the dear children
In Thy tender care,
And fit us for heaven,
To live with Thee there.

Coventry Carol

Words and music: Traditional

Lully, lullay, thou little tiny Child,
Bye, bye, lully, lullay.

1. O sisters too, how may we do,
For to preserve this day,
This poor youngling for whom we do sing
Bye, bye, lully, lullay.

2. Herod, the king, in his raging,
Chargèd he hath this day
His men of might, in his own sight,
All young children to slay.

3. That woe is me, poor Child for Thee!
And ever mourn and say,
For thy parting neither say nor sing,
Bye, bye, lully, lullay.

Deck the hall

Not too fast

Words and music: Traditional

1. Deck the halls with boughs of holly, *Fa la la la la, la la la la.*
'Tis the season to be jolly. *Fa la la la la, la la la la.*
Don we now our gay apparel, *Fa la la, la la la, la la la.*
Troll the ancient Yuletide carol. *Fa la la la la, la la la la.*

2. See the blazing Yule before us, *Fa la la...*
Strike the harp and join the chorus. *Fa la la...*
Follow me in merry measure, *Fa la la...*
While I tell of Yuletide treasure. *Fa la la...*

3. Fast away the old year passes, *Fa la la...*
Hail the new, ye lads and lasses. *Fa la la...*
Sing we joyous, all together, *Fa la la...*
Heedless of the wind and weather, *Fa la la...*

Ding dong! Merrily on high

Words: George Woodward
Music: Traditional

1. Ding dong! Merrily on high
In heav'n the bells are ringing.
Ding dong! Verily the sky
Is riv'n with angels singing:

Gloria, Hosanna in excelsis!

2. E'en so here below, below
Let steeple bells be swungen,
And *io, io, io,*
By priest and people sungen.

3. Pray you dutifully prime
Your matin chimes, ye ringers.
May you beautifully rhyme
Your evetime song, ye singers.

Gabriel's Message

Music: Traditional Basque
Words: Traditional Basque
Translation: Sabine Baring-Gould

Liltingly

1. The angel Gabriel from heaven came,
His wings as drifted snow, his eyes as flame;
"All hail," said he, "thou lowly maiden Mary,
Most highly favoured lady," Gloria!

2. "For know a blessed Mother thou shalt be,
All generations laud and honour thee,
Thy Son shall be Emmanuel, by seers foretold,
Most highly favoured lady," Gloria!

3. Then gentle Mary meekly bowed her head,
"To me be as it pleaseth God," she said,
"My soul shall laud and magnify his holy Name."
Most highly favoured lady, Gloria!

4. Of her, Emmanuel, the Christ, was born
in Bethlehem, all on a Christmas morn,
and Christian folk throughout the world will ever say:
"Most highly favoured lady," Gloria!

Gaudete!

Medieval carol,
from *Piae Cantiones*

Gaudete! Gaudete! Christus est natus
Ex Maria virgine: Gaudete!

1. Tempus ad est gratiae
Hoc quod optabamus;
Carmina laetitiae
Devote reddamus.

2. Deus homo factus est,
Natura mirante;
Mundus renovatus est
A Christo regnante.

3. Ezechielis porta
Clausa pertransitur;
Unde lux est orta,
Salus invenitur.

4. Ergo nostra concio
Psallat jam in lustro;
Benedicat Domino:
Salus regi nostro.

God rest ye merry gentlemen

Words and music: Traditional

1. God rest ye merry gentlemen,
Let nothing you dismay,
For Jesus Christ our Saviour
Was born on Christmas Day
To save us all from Satan's power
Long time had gone astray

O tidings of comfort and joy,
Comfort and joy,
O tidings of comfort and joy.

2. From God our heavenly Father
A blessed angel came
And unto certain shepherds
Brought tidings of the same;
How that in Bethlehem was born
The Son of God by name.

3. The shepherds at those tidings
Rejoiced much in mind,
And left their flocks a-feeding
In tempest, storm and wind.
And went to Bethlehem straightway,
This blessed Babe to find.

4. But when to Bethlehem they came,
Whereat this Infant lay
They found Him in a manger
Where oxen feed on hay.
His mother Mary kneeling
Unto the Lord did pray.

5. Now to the Lord sing praises
All you within this place,
And with true love and brotherhood
Each other now embrace;
This holy time of Christmas
All others doth deface.

Good King Wenceslas

Music: Traditional
Words: J. M. Neale

Moderately

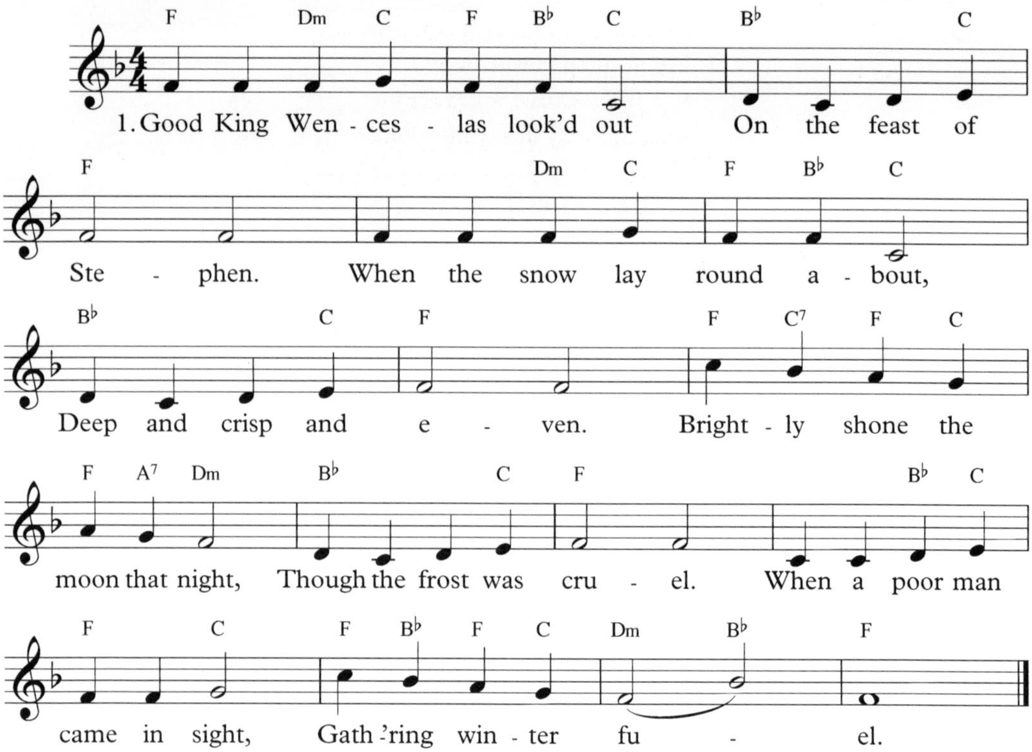

1. Good King Wenceslas look'd out
On the feast of Stephen.
When the snow lay round about,
Deep and crisp and even.
Brightly shone the moon that night,
Though the frost was cruel.
When a poor man came in sight,
Gath'ring winter fuel.

2. "Hither, page, and stand by me,
If though know'st it, telling.
Yonder peasant who is he?
Where and what his dwelling?"
"Sire, he lives a good league hence,
Underneath the mountain;
Right against the forest fence,
By St. Agnes' fountain."

3. "Bring me flesh and bring me wine,
Bring me pine logs hither;
Thou and I shall see him dine,
When we bear them thither."
Page and monarch forth they went,
Forth they went together,
Through the rude wind's wild lament,
And the bitter weather.

4. "Sire, the night is darker now,
And the wind blows stronger.
Fails my heart, I know not how,
I can go no longer."
"Mark my footsteps, good my page!
Tread thou in them boldly,
Thou shall find the winter's rage
Freeze thy blood less coldly."

5. In his master's steps he trod,
Where the snow lay dinted.
Heat was in the very sod
Which the saint had printed.
Therefore, Christian men, be sure,
Wealth or rank possessing;
Ye, who now will bless the poor
Shall yourselves find blessing.

Hark! The herald angels sing

Music: Felix Mendelssohn
Words: Charles Wesley

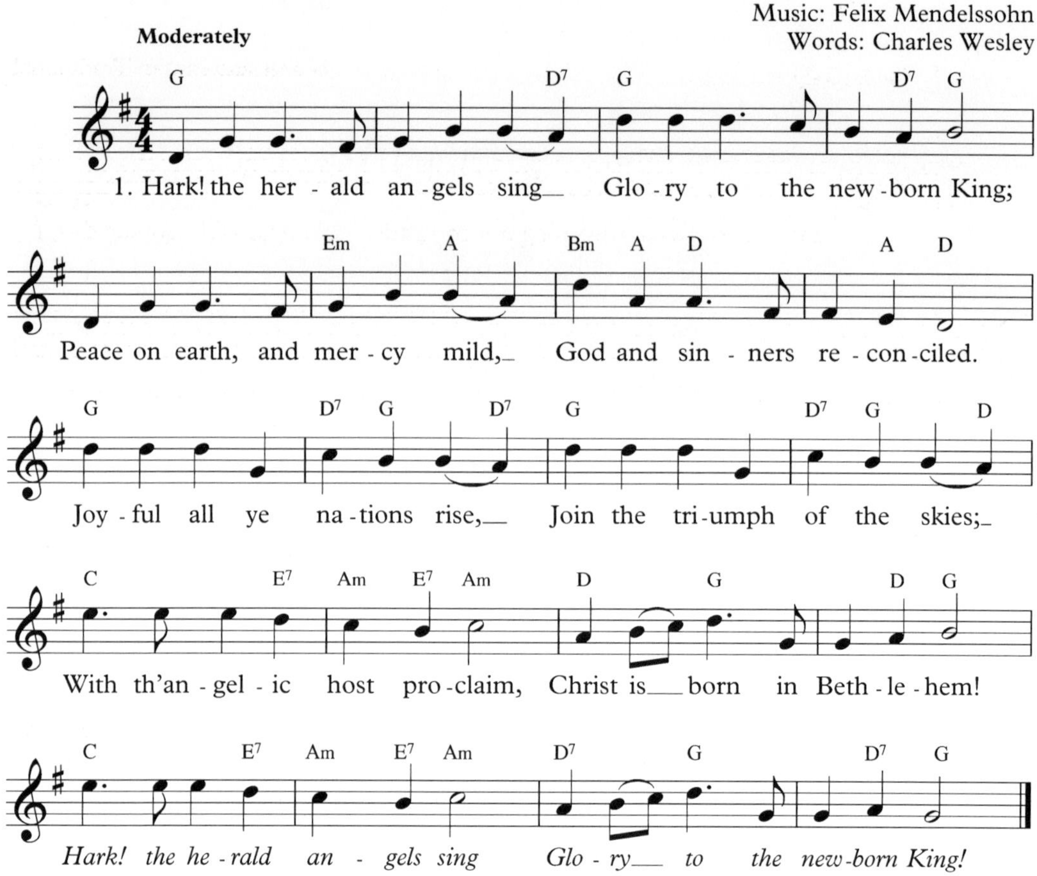

1. Hark! the herald angels sing
Glory to the new-born King;
Peace on earth, and mercy mild,
God and sinners reconciled.
Joyful all ye nations rise,
Join the triumph of the skies;
With th'angelic host proclaim,
Christ is born in Bethlehem!
Hark! The herald angels sing
Glory to the new-born King!

2. Christ by highest heav'n adored
Christ the everlasting Lord!
Late in time behold Him come,
Offspring of a Virgin's womb.
Veiled in flesh the Godhead see,
Hail the incarnate Deity.
Pleased as man with man to dwell,
Jesus, our Emmanuel.
Hark! The herald angels sing
Glory to the newborn King!

3. Hail the heav'n-born Prince of Peace!
Hail the Son of Righteousness!
Light and life to all He brings,
Ris'n with healing in His wings.
Mild He lays His glory by,
Born that man no more may die.
Born to raise the sons of earth,
Born to give them second birth.
Hark! The herald angels sing
Glory to the newborn King!

I saw three ships

Words and music: Traditional

Moderately

1. I saw three ships come sailing in
On Christmas day, on Christmas day;
I saw three ships come sailing in
On Christmas day in the morning.

2. And what was in those ships all three
On Christmas day, on Christmas day;
And what was in those ships all three
On Christmas day in the morning?

3. Our Saviour Christ and His lady,
On Christmas day, on Christmas day;
Our Saviour Christ and His lady,
On Christmas day in the morning.

4. Pray, whither sailed those ships all three
On Christmas day, on Christmas day;
Pray, whither sailed those ships all three
On Christmas day in the morning?

5. O they sailed into Bethlehem
On Christmas day, on Christmas day;
O they sailed into Bethlehem
On Christmas day in the morning.

6. And all the bells on earth shall ring
On Christmas day, on Christmas day;
And all the bells on earth shall ring
On Christmas day in the morning.

7. And all the angels in heaven shall sing
On Christmas day, on Christmas day;
And all the angels in heaven shall sing
On Christmas day in the morning.

8. And all the souls on earth shall sing
On Christmas day, on Christmas day;
And all the souls on earth shall sing
On Christmas day in the morning.

9. Then let us all rejoice amain
On Christmas day, on Christmas day;
Then let us all rejoice amain
On Christmas day in the morning.

In dulci jubilo

Joyfully

Words and music: Traditional

1. *In dulci jubilo*
Let us our homage show.
Our heart's joy reclineth,
In praesepio,
And like a bright star shineth,
Matris in gremio,
Alpha es et O!

2. *O Jesu parvule,*
My heart is sore for Thee,
Hear me, I beseech Thee,
O puer optime,
My praying let it reach Thee!
O princeps gloriae.
Trahe me post te.

3. *O patris caritas!*
O Nati lenitas!
Deeply were we stained,
Per nostra crimina,
But Thou for us hast gained,
Coelorum gaudia,
Qualis gloria!

4. *Ubi sunt gaudia,*
If that they be not there?
There are angels singing,
Nova cantica;
And there the bells are ringing,
In Regis curia.
O that we were there!

In the bleak mid-winter

Music: Gustav Holst
Words: Christina Rossetti

Moderately

1. In the bleak midwinter
Frosty wind made moan;
Earth stood hard as iron,
Water like a stone.
Snow had fallen snow on snow, snow on snow.
In the bleak midwinter long ago.

2. Our God, heav'n cannot hold him,
Nor earth sustain,
Heav'n and earth shall flee away
When He comes to reign.
In the bleak midwinter a stable place sufficed
The Lord God Almighty Jesus Christ.

3. Enough for him, whom cherubim
Worship night and day,
A breastful of milk
And a mangerful of hay.
Enough for Him, whom angels fall down before,
The ox and ass and camel which adore.

4. Angels and archangels
May have gathered there;
Cherubim and seraphim
Thronged the air.
But only His mother in her maiden bliss
Worshipped the Beloved with a kiss.

5. What can I give him
Poor as I am?
If I were a shepherd
I would bring a lamb.
If I were a wise man I would do my part;
Yet what I can I give Him, give my heart.

It came upon the midnight clear

Music: Adapted from an English melody
Words: Edmund H. Sears

Moderately

1. It came upon the midnight clear,
That glorious song of old,
From angels bending near the earth,
To touch their harps of gold;
"Peace on the earth, goodwill to men,
From Heaven's eternal King."
The world in solemn stillness lay,
To hear the angels sing.

2. Still through the cloven skies they come
With peaceful wings unfurled,
And still their heavenly music floats
O'er all the weary world;
Above its sad and lowly plains,
They bend on hovering wing,
And ever o'er its Babel sounds
The blessèd angels sing.

3. Yet with the woes of sin and strife
The world has suffered long;
Beneath the angel strain have rolled
Two thousand years of wrong;
And man, at war with man, hears not
The love-song which they bring;
O hush the noise, ye men of strife
And hear the angels sing.

4. For lo! the days are hastening on,
By prophet-bards foretold,
When with the ever-circling years
Comes round the age of gold;
When peace shall over all the earth
Its ancient splendours fling,
And the whole world send back the song
Which now the angels sing.

Joy to the world

Music: George Frideric Handel
Words: Isaac Watts

1. Joy to the world!
The Lord is come;
Let earth receive her King;
Let ev'ry heart prepare Him room,
And heav'n and nature sing,
And heav'n and nature sing,
And heav'n, and heav'n and nature sing.

2. Joy to the world!
The Saviour reigns.
Let men their songs employ,
While field and floods, rocks, hills and plains,
Repeat the sounding joy,
Repeat the sounding joy,
Repeat, repeat the sounding joy.

3. He rules the world!
With truth and grace,
And makes the nations prove
The glories of His righteousness,
And wonders of His love,
And wonders of His love,
And wonders, wonders of His love.

Jingle Bells

Words and music: James Lord Pierpont

1. Dashing through the snow
In a one-horse open sleigh,
O'er the fields we go,
Laughing all the way.
Bells on bobtails ring,
Making spirits bright,
What fun it is to ride and sing
A sleighing song tonight.

Jingle bells, jingle bells,
Jingle all the way.
Oh what fun it is to ride
In a one-horse open sleigh.
Jingle bells, jingle bells,
Jingle all the way.
Oh what fun it is to ride
In a one-horse open sleigh.

2. A day or two ago
I thought I'd take a ride,
And soon Miss Fanny Bright
Was seated by my side.
The horse was lean and lank,
Misfortune seemed his lot,
He got into a drifted bank
And then we got upsot.

3. A day or two ago,
The story I must tell,
I went out on the snow
And on my back I fell.
A gent was riding by,
In a one-horse open sleigh,
He laughed as there I sprawling lay,
But quickly drove away.

4. Now the ground is white,
Go it while you're young;
Take the girls tonight
And sing this sleighing song.
Just get a bobtailed bay,
Two forty for his speed,
Hitch him to an open sleigh
And, crack, you'll take the lead.

Long ago, prophets knew

Music: From *Piae Cantiones*
Words: Fred Pratt Green

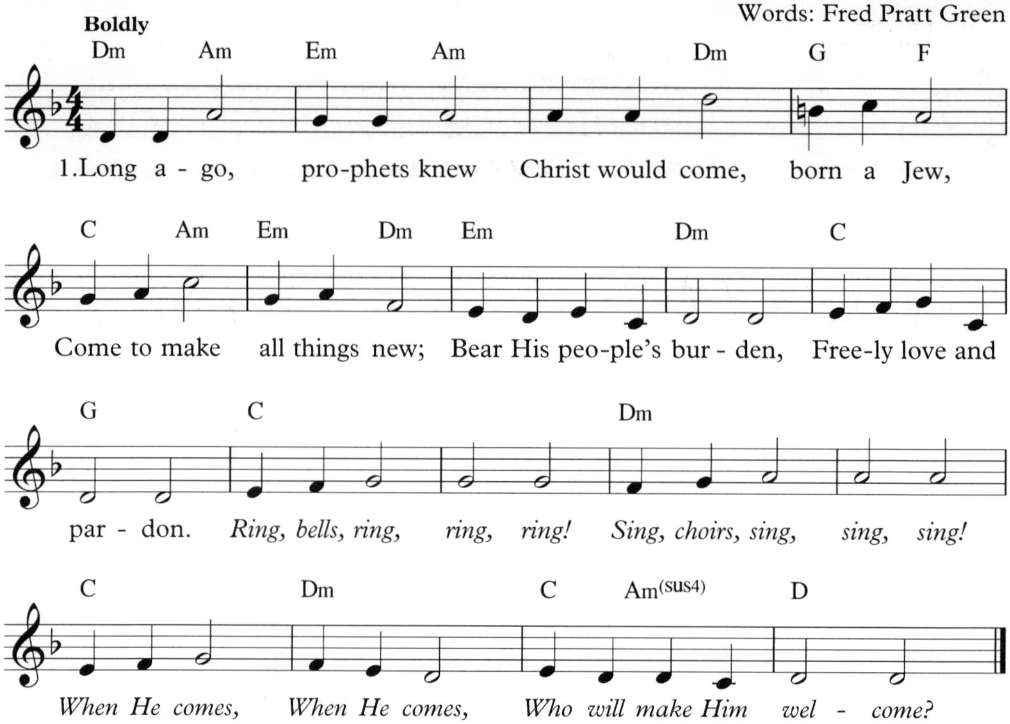

1. Long ago, prophets knew
Christ would come, born a Jew,
Come to make all things new;
Bear His people's burden,
Freely love and pardon.

Ring, bells, ring, ring, ring!
Sing, choirs, sing, sing, sing!
When He comes,
When He comes,
Who will make Him welcome?

2. God in time, God in man,
This is God's timeless plan:
He will come, as a man,
Born himself of woman,
God divinely human:

3. Mary hail! Though afraid,
She believed, she obeyed.
In her womb, God is laid:
Till the time expected,
Nurtured and protected.

4. Journey ends! Where afar
Bethlehem shines, like a star,
Stable door stands ajar.
Unborn Son of Mary,
Saviour, do not tarry!

Ring, bells, ring, ring, ring!
Sing, choirs, sing, sing, sing!
When He comes,
When He comes,
We will make Him welcome!

Traditional Music
Words by Fred Pratt Green

O Christmas Tree

Words and music: Traditional

1. O Christmas Tree! O Christmas Tree!
Thy leaves are so unchanging;
O Christmas Tree! O Christmas Tree!
Thy leaves are so unchanging;
Not only green when summer's here,
But also when 'tis cold and drear.
O Christmas Tree! O Christmas Tree!
Thy leaves are so unchanging!

2. O Christmas Tree! O Christmas Tree!
Much pleasure thou can'st give me;
O Christmas Tree! O Christmas Tree!
Much pleasure thou can'st give me;
How often has the Christmas tree
Afforded me the greatest glee!
O Christmas Tree! O Christmas Tree!
Much pleasure thou can'st give me.

3. O Christmas Tree! O Christmas Tree!
Thy candles shine so brightly!
O Christmas Tree! O Christmas Tree!
Thy candles shine so brightly!
From base to summit, gay and bright,
There's only splendour for the sight.
O Christmas Tree! O Christmas Tree!
Thy candles shine so brightly!

4. O Christmas Tree! O Christmas Tree!
How richly God hath decked thee!
O Christmas Tree! O Christmas Tree!
How richly God hath decked thee!
Thou bidst us true and faithful be,
And trust in God unchangingly.
O Christmas Tree! O Christmas Tree!
How richly God has decked thee!

O come all ye faithful

Words and music: John Francis Wade

2. God of God,
Light of light,
Lo! He abhors not the Virgin's womb;
Very God, begotten not created.

3. See how the shepherds,
Summoned to his cradle,
Leaving their flocks, draw nigh in lowly fear;
We too will thither bend our joyful footsteps.

4. Lo! star-led chieftains,
Magi, Christ adoring,
Offer him frankincense, gold and myrrh;
We to the Christ-child bring our hearts oblations.

5. Child, for us sinners
Poor and in the manger,
We would embrace thee, with love and awe;
Who would not love thee, loving us so dearly?

6. Sing, choirs of angels,
Sing in exultation,
Sing, all ye citizens of heav'n above;
Glory to God in the highest.

7. Yea, Lord, we greet Thee,
Born on Christmas morning,
Jesu, to Thee be glory given;
Word of the father, now in flesh appearing.

O come, O come Emmanuel!

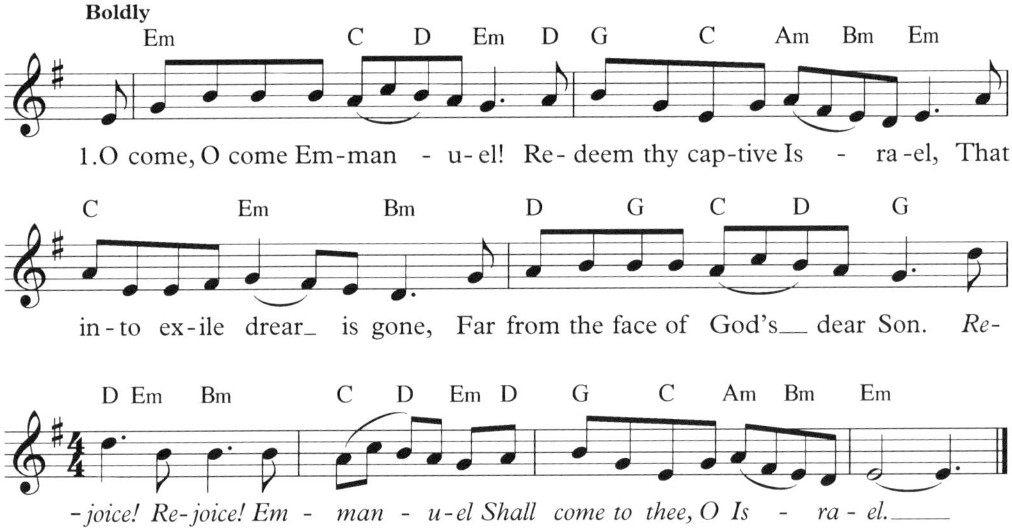

1. O come, O come, Emmanuel!
Redeem thy captive Israel,
That into exile drear is gone
Far from the face of God's dear Son.

Rejoice! Rejoice! Emmanuel
Shall come to thee, O Israel.

2. O come, thou Branch of Jesse! draw
The quarry from the lion's claw;
From the dread caverns of the grave,
From nether hell thy people save.

3. O come, O come, thou Dayspring bright!
Pour on our souls thy healing light;
Dispel the long night's lingering gloom,
And pierce the shadows of the tomb.

4. O come, thou Lord of David's Key!
The royal door fling wide and free;
Safeguard for us the heav'nward road,
And bar the way to death's abode.

5. O come, O come, Adonaï,
Who in thy glorious majesty
From that high mountain clothed with awe
Gavest thy folk the elder law.

O holy night

Music: Adolphe Adam
Words: Placide Cappeau
Translation: John Sullivan Dwight

Moderately

1. O holy night! The stars are brightly shining,
It is the night of our dear Saviour's birth.
Long lay the world in sin and error pining,
Till He appeared and the soul felt its worth.
A thrill of hope the weary world rejoices,
For yonder breaks a new and glorious morn.

Fall on your knees! O hear the angels' voices!
O night divine, O night when Christ was born;
O night divine, O night, O night Divine!

2. Led by the light of faith serenely beaming,
With glowing hearts by His cradle we stand.
So led by light of a star sweetly gleaming,
Here come the wise men from th'Orient land.
The King of Kings lay thus in lowly manger;
In all our trials born to be our friend.

He knows our need, He guardeth us from danger,
Behold your King! Before Him lowly bend!
Behold your King, Before Him lowly bend!

O little one sweet

Music: Traditional German tune
Words: Traditional, trans. Percy Dearmer

1. O little one sweet,
O little one mild,
Thy Father's purpose thou hast fulfilled;
Thou cam'st from heav'n to mortal ken,
Equal to be with us poor men,
O little one sweet,
O little one mild.

2. O little one sweet,
O little one mild,
With joy Thou hast the whole world filled;
Thou camest here from heav'n's domain,
To bring men comfort in their pain,
O little one sweet,
O little one mild.

3. O little one sweet,
O little one mild,
In Thee Love's beauties are all distilled;
Then light in us Thy love's bright flame
That we may give Thee back the same.
O little one sweet,
O little one mild.

4. O little one sweet,
O little one mild,
Help us to do as Thou hast willed.
Lo, all we have belongs to Thee!
Ah, keep us in our fealty!
O little one sweet,
O little one mild.

O little town of Bethlehem

Music: Traditional
Words: Phillips Brooks

Moderately

1. O little town of Bethlehem,
How we still see thee lie.
Above thy deep and dreamless sleep,
The silent stars go by.
Yet in thy dark streets shineth
The everlasting Light.
The hopes and fears of all the years
Are met in thee tonight.

2. O morning stars, together
Proclaim the holy birth,
And praises sing to God the King,
And peace to men on earth.
For Christ is born of Mary
And gathered all above,
While mortals sleep, the angels keep
Their watch of wondering love.

3. How silently, how silently
The wondrous gift is given!
So God imparts to human hearts
The blessings of His heaven.
No ear may hear His coming,
But in this world of sin,
Where meek souls will receive Him, still
The dear Christ enters in.

4. O holy child of Bethlehem
Descend to us we pray.
Cast out our sin and enter in,
Be born in us today.
We hear the Christmas angels
The great glad tidings tell.
O come to us, abide with us,
Our Lord Emmanuel.

Of the father's heart begotten

Music: Traditional
Words: Aurelius Prudentius

1. Of the Father's heart begotten
Ere the world from chaos rose,
He is Alpha: from that Fountain,
All that is and hath been flows;
He is Omega, of all things,
Yet to come the mystic Close,
Evermore and evermore.

2. By his word was all created;
He commanded and 'twas done;
Earth and sky and boundless ocean,
Universe of three in one,
All that sees the moon's soft radiance,
All that breathes beneath the sun,
Evermore and evermore.

3. He assumed this mortal body,
Frail and feeble, doomed to die,
That the race from dust created
Might not perish utterly,
Which the dreadful Law had sentenced
In the depths of hell to lie,
Evermore and evermore.

4. O how blest that wondrous birthday,
When the Maid the curse retrieved,
Brought to birth mankind's salvation,
By the Holy Ghost conceived,
And the Babe, the world's Redeemer,
In her loving arms received,
Evermore and evermore.

5. This is He, whom seer and sybil
Sang in ages long gone by;
This is He of old revealed
In the page of prophecy;
Lo! He comes, the promised Saviour;
Let the world His praises cry!
Evermore and evermore.

6. Sing, ye heights of heaven, His praises;
Angels and Archangels, sing!
Wheresoe'er ye be, ye faithful,
Let your joyous anthems ring,
Every tongue his name confessing,
Countless voices answering,
Evermore and evermore.

Once in royal David's city

Music: Henry Gauntlett
Words: C. F. Alexander

Majestically

1. Once in royal Davids city,
Stood a lowly cattle shed,
Where a mother laid her Baby,
In a manger for His bed:
Mary was that mother mild,
Jesus Christ, her little Child.

2. He came down to earth from heaven,
Who is God and Lord of all;
And His shelter was a stable,
And His cradle was a stall;
With the poor and mean and lowly,
Lived on earth our Saviour holy.

3. And through all His wondrous childhood
He would honour and obey;
Love and watch the lowly Maiden
In whose gentle arms He lay;
Christian children all must be
Mild, obedient, good as He.

4. For He is our childhood's pattern,
Day by day like us He grew;
He was little, weak and helpless,
Tears and smiles like us He knew;
And He feeleth for our sadness,
And He shareth in our gladness.

5. And our eyes at last shall see Him,
Through his own redeeming love;
For that Child so dear and gentle
Is our Lord in heaven above;
And He leads His children on
To the place where He has gone.

6. Not in that poor lowly stable,
With the oxen standing by;
We shall see Him, but in heaven,
Set at God's right hand on high;
When like stars His children crowned,
All in white shall wait around.

Past three o' clock

Music: Traditional
Words: George Woodward

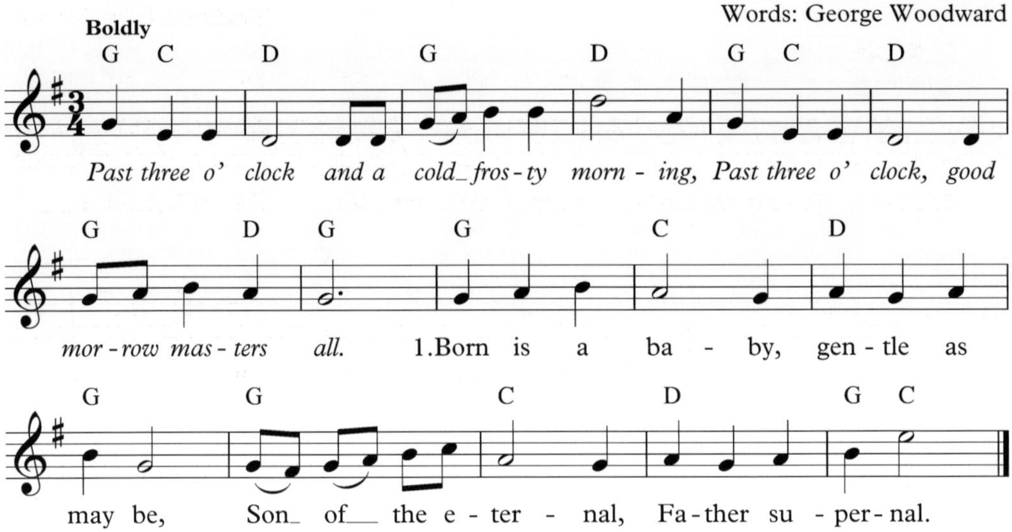

Past three o'clock and a cold frosty morning,
Past three o'clock, good morrow masters all.

1. Born is a baby, gentle as may be,
Son of the eternal, Father supernal.

2. Seraph quire singeth, angel bell ringeth,
Hark how they rhyme it, time it and chime it.

3. Mid earth rejoices hearing such voices,
Ne'ertofore so well carolling Nowell.

4. Hind o'er the pearly dewy lawn early,
Seek the high Stranger laid in a manger.

5. Cheese from the dairy, bring it for Mary,
And not for money, butter or honey.

6. Light out the star-land leadeth from far land,
Princes to meet Him, worship and greet Him.

7. Myrrh from full coffer, incense they offer,
Nor is the golden nugget withholden.

8. Thus then I pray you, up sirs nor stay you,
Till ye confess Him, likewise and bless Him.

Rocking

Traditional Czech carol

1. Little Jesus, sweetly sleep, do not stir,
We will lend a coat of fur.
We will rock you, rock you, rock you,
We will rock you, rock you, rock you.
See the fur to keep you warm,
Snugly round your tiny form.

2. Mary's little baby, sleep, sweetly sleep,
Sleep in comfort, slumber deep.
We will rock you, rock you, rock you,
We will rock you, rock you, rock you.
We will serve you all we can,
Darling, darling little man.

See amid the winter's snow

Music: John Goss
Words: Edward Caswell

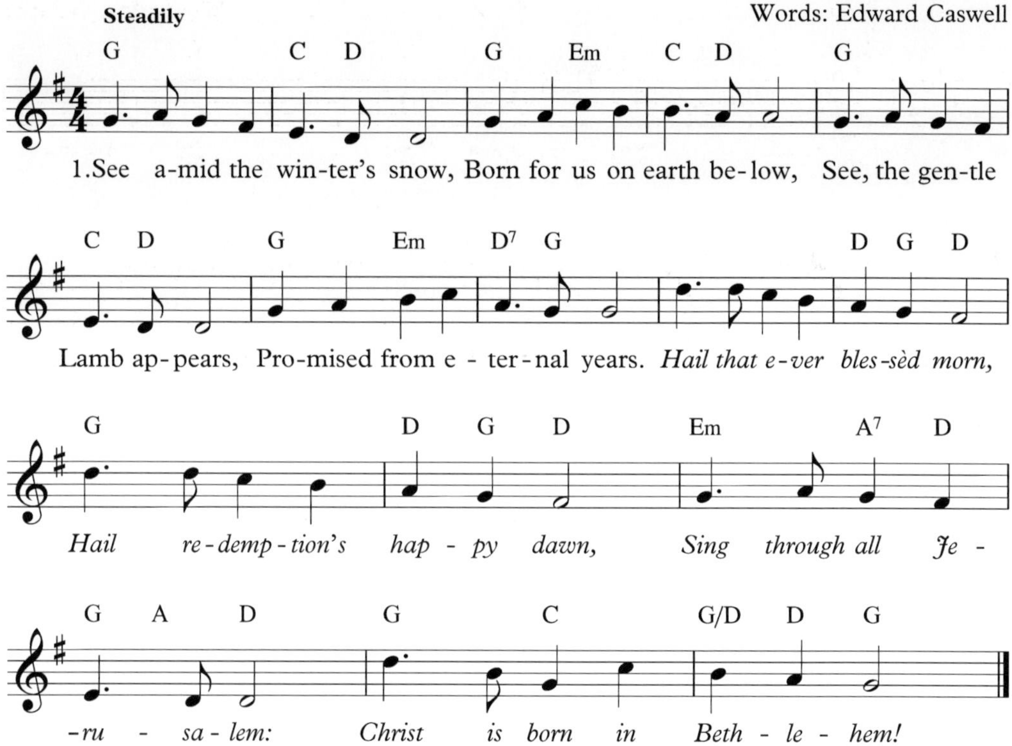

1. See amid the winter's snow,
Born for us on earth below,
See, the gentle Lamb appears,
Promised from eternal years.

Hail that ever blessèd morn,
Hail redemption's happy dawn,
Sing through all Jerusalem:
Christ is born in Bethlehem!

2. Lo, within a manger lies
He who built the starry skies;
He who, throned in height sublime,
Sits amid the cherubim.

3. Say, you holy shepherds, say,
Tell your joyful news today.
Why have you now left your sheep
On the lonely mountain steep?

4. "As we watched at dead of night,
Lo, we saw a wondrous light;
Angels singing 'Peace on earth'
Told us of the Saviour's birth."

5. Sacred Infant, all divine,
What a tender love was Thine,
Thus to come from highest bliss
Down to such a world as this.

6. Teach, O teach us, holy Child,
By Thy face so meek and mild,
Teach us to resemble Thee,
In Thy sweet humility.

Silent night

Music: Franz Gruber
Words: Joseph Mohr

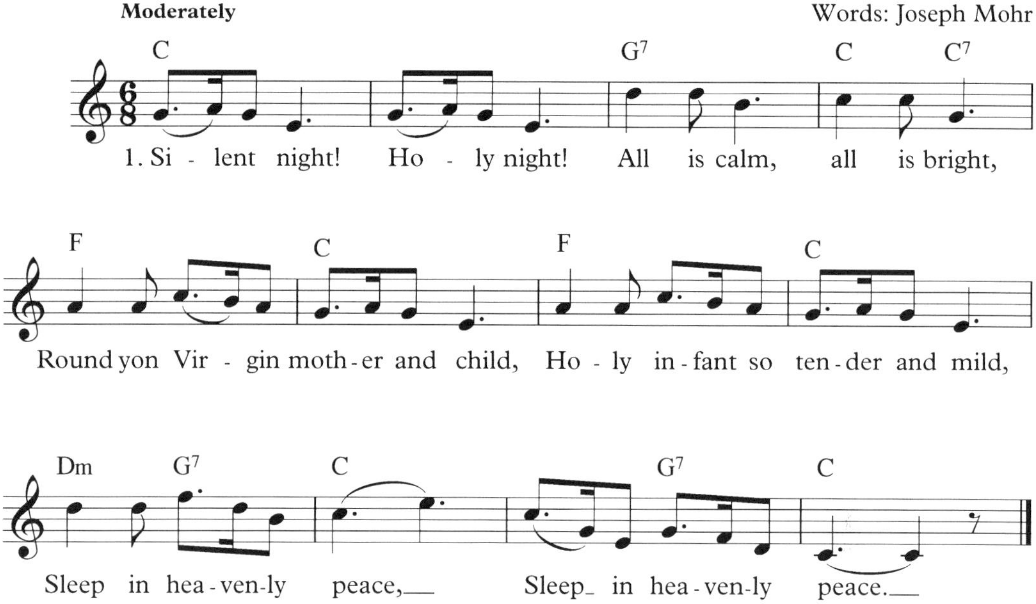

1. Silent night! Holy night!
All is calm, all is bright,
Round yon virgin mother and child,
Holy infant so tender and mild,
Sleep in heavenly peace,
Sleep in heavenly peace.

2. Silent night! Holy night!
Shepherds quail at the sight;
Glories stream from heaven afar,
Heavenly hosts sing Alleluia!
Christ the Saviour is born,
Christ the Saviour is born.

3. Silent night! Holy night!
Son of God, love's pure light!
Radiant beams Thy holy face
With the dawn of saving grace;
Jesus, Lord, at Thy birth,
Jesus, Lord, at Thy birth.

Still, still, still

Words and music: Traditional

1. Still, still, still, let all the world be still.
For Mary lays her Son to rest,
Sing to Him softly at her breast;
Still, still, still, let all the world be still.

2. Sleep, sleep, sleep, my dearest baby, sleep;
The angels all rejoice and sing,
Heav'n for your delight shall ring;
Sleep, sleep, sleep, my dearest baby, sleep;

3. Joy, joy, joy, my heart is filled with joy.
The God of love has left His throne,
Made this humble world His home;
Joy, joy, joy, my heart is filled with joy.

Sussex Carol

Words and music: Traditional

1. On Christmas night all christians sing
To hear the news the angels bring.
On Christmas night all christians sing
To hear the news the angels bring.
News of great joy, news of great mirth,
News of our merciful King's birth.

2. Then why should men on earth be so sad,
Since our Redeemer made us glad,
Then why should men on earth be so sad,
Since our Redeemer made us glad,
When from our sin He set us free,
All for to gain our liberty?

3. When sin departs before His grace,
Then life and health come in its place.
When sin departs before His grace,
Then life and health come in its place.
Angels and men with joy may sing,
All for to see the newborn King.

4. All out of darkness we have light,
Which made the angels sing this night.
All out of darkness we have light,
Which made the angels sing this night.
Glory to God and peace to men,
Now and for evermore, Amen.

The first Nowell

Moderately

Words and music: Traditional

1. The first Nowell, the angels did say,
Was to certain poor shepherds in fields as they lay;
In fields where they lay, keeping their sheep,
On a cold winter's night that was so deep:

Nowell, Nowell, Nowell, Nowell.
Born is the King of Israel!

2. They lookèd up and saw a star
Shining in the East beyond them far,
And to the earth it gave great light,
And so it continued both day and night.

3. And by the light of that same star
Three wise men came from country far
To seek for a king was their intent,
And to follow the star wheresoever it went.

4. This star drew nigh to the north-west,
O'er Bethlehem it took its rest,
And there it did both stop and stay,
Right over the place where Jesus lay.

5. Then let us all with one accord
Sing praises to our heavenly Lord,
That hath made Heaven and Earth of nought,
And with His blood mankind hath bought.

The holly and the ivy

Moderately

Words and music: Traditional

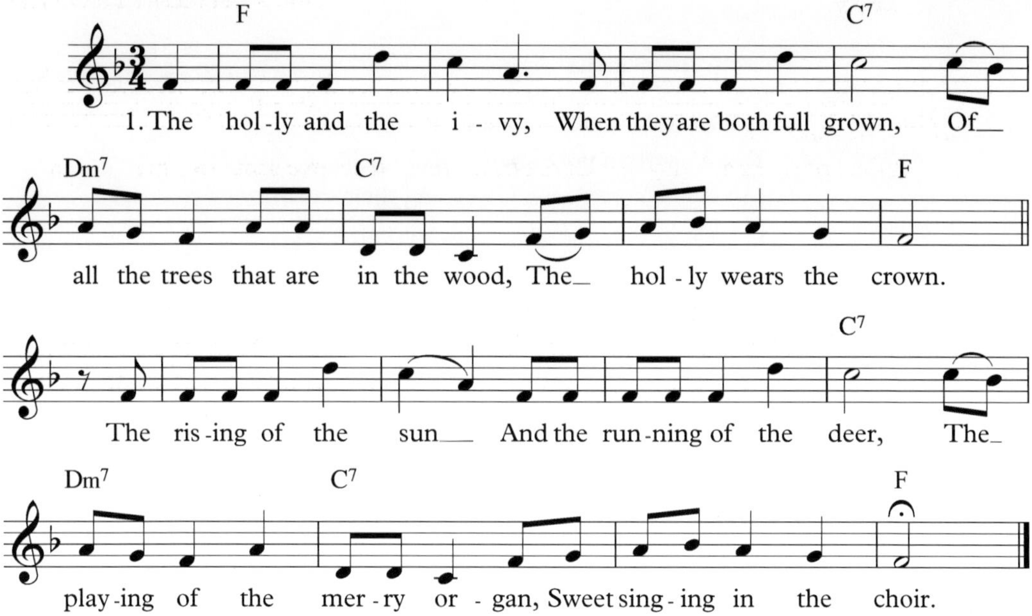

1. The holly and the ivy,
When they are both full grown,
Of all the trees that are in the wood,
The holly bears the crown.

The rising of the sun,
And the running of the deer,
The playing of the merry organ,
Sweet singing of the choir.

2. The holly bears a blossom
As white as any flower;
And Mary bore sweet Jesus Christ
To be our sweet saviour.

3. The holly bears a berry
As red as any blood;
And Mary bore sweet Jesus Christ
To do poor sinners good.

4. The holly bears a prickle
As sharp as any thorn;
And Mary bore sweet Jesus Christ
On Christmas Day in the morn.

5. The holly bears a bark
As bitter as any gall;
And Mary bore sweet Jesus Christ
For to redeem us all.

6. The holly and the ivy,
When they are both full grown,
Of all the trees that are in the wood,
The holly bears the crown.

The Twelve Days of Christmas

Lively

Words and music: Traditional

F Bb F/C C7 F C7
part - ridge in a pear tree. 4. On the
F C7 F
fourth day of Christ - mas my true love sent to me:
C7 Gm C7 Gm C7 Gm
four col - ly birds, three French hens, two tur - tle doves and a
F Bb F/C C7 F C7
part - ridge in a pear tree. 5. On the
F C7 F
fifth day of Christ - mas my true love sent to me:
Dm7 G7 C7 F Bb
five gold rings. Four col - ly birds, three French hens,

G7 C7 F B♭ F/C C7 F C7
two_ tur - tle doves and a part - ridge_ in a pear tree. 6. On the
F C7 F
sixth day of Christ - mas my true love sent to me:
seventh day of Christ - mas my true love sent to me:
eighth day of Christ - mas my true love sent to me:
ninth day of Christ - mas my true love sent to me:
tenth day of Christ - mas my true love sent to me:
eleventh day of Christ - mas my true love sent to me:
twelfth day of Christ - mas my true love sent to me:
C7 Gm
six geese a - lay - ing,
seven swans a - swim - ming,(to 6)
eight maids a - milk - ing, (to 7)
nine drum - mers drum - ming,(to 8)
ten pip - ers pip - ing, (to 9)
eleven la - dies danc - ing, (to 10)
twelve lords a - leap - ing, (to 11)
Dm7 G7 C7 F B♭
five gold_ rings, four_ col - ly birds, three French hens,
6 times D.S.
Last time
G7 C7 F B♭ F/C C7 F (7-12.) F
two_ tur tle doves, and a part - ridge in a pear tree. On the tree.

Unto us is born a Son

Music: Traditional
Words: George Woodward

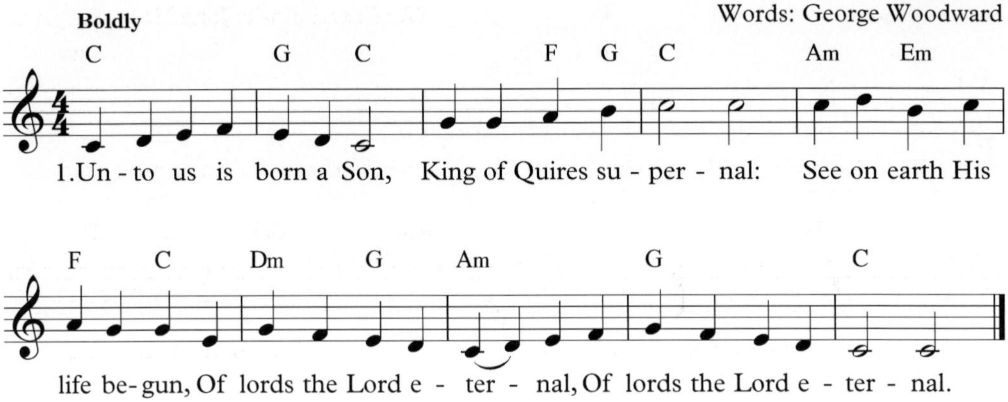

1. Unto us is born a Son,
King of Quires supernal:
See on earth His life begun,
Of lords the Lord eternal,
Of lords the Lord eternal.

2. Christ, from heav'n descending low
Comes on earth a stranger;
Ox and ass their owner know,
Be cradled in the manger,
Be cradled in the manger.

3. This did Herod sore affray,
And grievously bewilder,
So he gave the word to slay,
And slew the little childer,
And slew the little childer.

4. Of His love and mercy mild,
This the Christmas story;
And O that Mary's gentle child
Might lead us up to glory!
Might lead us up to glory!

5. O and A, and A and O,
Cum cantibus in choro,
Let our merry organ go,
Benedicamus Domino,
Benedicamus Domino.

We three kings

1. We three kings of Orient are,
Bearing gifts we traverse afar,
Field and fountain, moor and mountain,
Following yonder star.

O Star of wonder, star of night,
Star with royal beauty bright,
Westward leading, still proceeding,
Guide us to thy perfect light.

2. Born a King on Bethlehem plain,
Gold I bring to crown Him again,
King forever, ceasing never,
Over us all to reign.

3. Frankincense to offer have I,
Incense owns a Deity nigh,
Prayer and praising, all men raising,
Worship Him, God most high.

4. Myrrh is mine, its bitter perfume
Breathes of life of gathering gloom,
Sorrowing, sighing, bleeding, dying,
Sealed in the stone-cold tomb.

5. Glorious now behold Him arise,
King and God and Sacrifice;
Alleluia, Alleluia,
Earth to heav'n replies.

We wish you a merry Christmas

Words and music: Traditional

1. We wish you a merry Christmas,
We wish you a merry Christmas,
We wish you a merry Christmas,
And a happy New Year!

Good tidings we bring to you and your kin;
We wish you a merry Christmas and a happy New Year!

2. Now bring us some figgy pudding,
Now bring us some figgy pudding,
Now bring us some figgy pudding,
And bring some out here!

3. For we all like figgy pudding,
We all like figgy pudding,
We all like figgy pudding,
So bring some out here!

4. And we won't go until we've got some,
We won't go until we've got some,
We won't go until we've got some,
So bring some out here!

While shepherds watched their flocks

Music: Traditional
Words: Nahum Tate

Moderately

1. While shepherds watched their flocks by night,
All seated on the ground,
The angel of the Lord came down
And glory shone around.

2. "Fear not," said he, for mighty dread
Had seized their troubled minds;
"Glad tidings of great joy I bring,
To you and all mankind."

3. "To you in David's town this day
Is born of David's line
A Saviour, who is Christ the Lord,
And this shall be the sign."

4. "The heavenly Babe you there shall find
To human view displayed,
All meanly wrapped in swathing bands,
And in a manger laid!"

5. Thus spake the Seraph; and forthwith
Appeared a shining throng
Of angels praising God, who thus
Addressed their joyful song.

6. "All glory be to God on high,
And on the earth be peace.
Goodwill henceforth from heaven to men,
Begin and never cease."

1 2 3 4 5 6 7 8 9